CW00848332

MY DNA DIARY

SICKLE CELL ANAEMIA

(Genetics for Kids)

Written by Lisa Mullan
Illustrated by Neil Chapman

Dinky Press Ltd

First Published in Great Britain 2019
by Dinky Press Ltd

ISBN 978-1-9164550-6-1

Text Copyright © Lisa Mullan 2019
Illustration Copyright © Neil Chapman 2019

All rights reserved. No part of this publication may be reproduced,
stored in or introduced into a retrieval system, or transmitted,
in any form, or by any means (electronic, mechanical,
photocopying, recording or otherwise) without the prior
written permission of the publisher.

The right of Lisa Mullan to be identified as the author of this work has been
asserted in accordance with the Copyright, Designs and Patents Act 1988

British Library Cataloguing-in-Publication Data
A catalogue record for this book is available from the British Library

https://www.dinkyamigos.com

Dedicated to everyone who lives with Sickle Cell Anaemia

Hi, I'm Alina.

You may not know this, but I am a
part of you. A tiny part that you can't
even see. What I do with my life might
affect yours.

Some people have Sickle Cell Anaemia.

Their red blood cells change shape and get
stuck, so they can't deliver oxygen to their
bodies. This causes pain and exhaustion.

Sickle Cell Anaemia is an illness that you are
born with.

It's inherited, which means that it has
something to do with me – and I'd like to
explain.

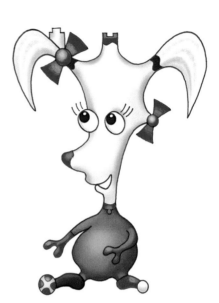

Welcome to

My DNA Diary: Sickle Cell Anaemia

Your life starts at conception. You have officially been created.
It's my job to make you the person you will become.

But I'm not doing this alone. I have my best friend Tristan.

There's Crispin and Gina too.

We also have loads of cousins. There are **billions** of them (literally).
We all look the same though, so it's hard to tell us apart.

We are all individuals – but
most people don't know
that because we are too
small for anyone to see. So
they group us together and
call us

DNA.

We call ourselves the **Dinky Amigos**. Your **Mum** and **Dad** have just given us to you.

Your Mum gives you one Dinky Amigos family.

Your Dad gives you a second Dinky Amigos family.

Scientists call this **DIPLOID**. This means you have 2 copies of your DNA: One copy from each parent.

A single Dinky Amigos family could do the job, but it's nice to have a backup — just in case.

In nine months' time you will be born. It's not long and we've got loads to do before then.

Before we go any further, I would just like to get something **straight**.

We are really, really, really tiny.

So tiny that you can't see us.
(Neither can anyone else!)

There are people called scientists who try to work out what we do.

As they can't see us either, scientists make us do loads of things they can see.

They call these experiments.

When they find something out, they **invent** a name for it. Sometimes, to be really precise, they use Greek words.

There are loads of these invented names.

I'll write them **LIKE THIS** and tell you what they mean because some are really long and sound like gobbledegook. I'll also explain them in a glossary at the back of this book.

We all live in a little village known as a **cell**.

Both Dinky Amigos families have to share a single area in the cell called the **nucleus**. It's a bit of a squash.

The rest of the cell is really full with all the other things it needs to keep you alive and healthy. There is no room for anything else.

Each cell has its own rules, its own food and power supply and a specific job to do.

Dinky Amigo Rules

You must do as
you are told

We will tell you
what to do

Dinky Amigos make up
those rules.

We are very strict!

You start life as just a single cell. You will have **trillions** of cells by the time you are born. There has to be copies of both Dinky Amigos families in nearly every single one!

There's not just one kind of cell, either. There are about 200 separate types. They all have a specific job to do (and each job needs different rules).

The type of cell that we help make the rules for is called an **ERYTHROCYTE**.

Most people call it a **red blood cell**.

The job of our red blood cell is to move **OXYGEN** from your lungs (where you breathe it in) to every other part of your body.

(If you have ever accidentally cut yourself, you might have seen our erythrocytes taking oxygen around the body. They make your blood look bright red.)

There are trillions of red blood cells in your body.

Each red blood cell is flat with a big curvy dent (like the eating side of a spoon) in both sides. Scientists call this dent **concave**.

The red blood cells are a bit like the delivery services you might use to get food, parcels or medicine.

If some of the deliveries got delayed or didn't turn up, you might be waiting a long time.

If none of the deliveries turned up, you would eventually run out of the thing you were waiting for.

If this happens to the oxygen supplies in your body, it could cause damage to your **ORGANS** (which might make you ill).

There are too many of us in the nucleus of a cell to live in one house. So each Dinky Amigos family splits up into 23 different houses called **CHROMOSOMES**. We live at Number 11.

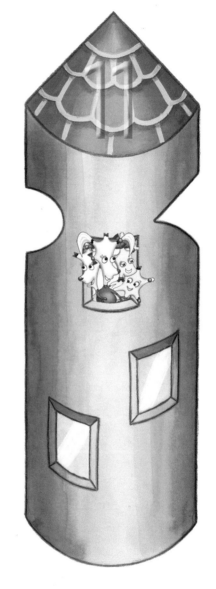

In each chromosome, some of the Dinky Amigos are split into groups called **GENES**.

Each gene is actually a set of instructions for a specific task

The gene we live in is called:

HaemogloBin
subunit
Beta

That's a bit of a mouthful, so everyone calls it **HBB** for short.

Our task in the HBB gene is to help the red blood cells keep your body alive.

These cells must transport oxygen from your lungs to everywhere else inside you. Everything in your body needs oxygen to work properly.

This includes really important organs like your

brain,
heart
and
kidneys.

To help your red blood cells transport oxygen, we make the instructions for a boat.

Our boat sits inside the red blood cell and is the perfect shape and size to help carry Oxygen around your body. But Oxygen won't get in by itself.

It needs something to play with.

Its favourite toy is **IRON** (sometimes written as Fe).

This is a metal found in the ground. It can be made into all sorts of things, such as: gates, benches, pots or tools. Iron also helps to make another metal called steel.

Iron isn't alive, so the Dinky Amigos can't make instructions for it.

Instead, we have to hope you **eat** enough iron for us to use in our boat.

Obviously you can't eat a bench, but meat, beans, nuts and green vegetables all have loads of iron in them.

(So does dark chocolate!)

Manufacturers also put iron into bread and cereals, so you can eat those, too.

The iron in these foods is stored in your body until we need it for our boat. Scientists and doctors call this store **FERRITIN**.

Scientists have given our boat a name. They call it **GLOBIN**. Sadly, globin isn't very interesting. But, once the iron is inside, our boat turns red and Oxygen gets really excited.

Scientists now give our boat a new name: **HAEMOGLOBIN** (you might see it written down as Hb).

It is the haemoglobin that delivers Oxygen from your lungs to the rest of your body. Iron is almost as important as we are!

How can we serve you, oh great one?

We don't build the haemoglobin boat ourselves, though. Instead, we give the cell builders precise instructions. They then build it exactly as we have told them to.

Nine months and trillions of cells later, you can make your entrance into the world.

All of those cells are spread out and joined together into a person shape – you!

But only a few of those cells are red blood cells.

Before you were born, your Mum let you use the Oxygen in **her** red blood cells. Her Oxygen didn't like our boat, though, and used another one instead. We didn't have much to do.

So at birth, you only have a cupful of blood.

But now we are really busy. By the time you are five, you will have lots more blood – nearly as much as an adult.

That much blood needs loads of red blood cells.

We need to make about 2 million of them every second.

Now that you have been born, we have to do everything. Your Mum can't lend you her Oxygen anymore.

It's just **you** and your **Dinky Amigos** from now on.

In lots of countries, doctors want a copy of us so they can check we are working properly.

They call it a **Heel Prick Test**.
A needle is inserted into your heel to take a sample of blood. Ouch!

Every single one of your Dinky Amigos are going to work their hardest to make sure you are the best person you can be.

That includes **us** in the **HBB** gene.

All blood cells are made in the middle of your bones in an area called the **Bone marrow**.

There are ten different types of blood cell – all with a specific job to do.

Our red blood cell is the only one that carries Oxygen around your body.

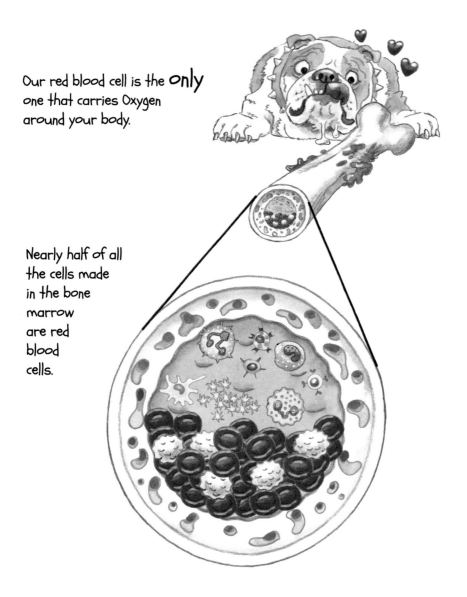

Nearly half of all the cells made in the bone marrow are red blood cells.

(Your pet dog might know that bone marrow is not only important, but tasty, too!)

We are really busy in the bone marrow, making instructions for the haemoglobin in all of those red blood cells.

But we have to be careful not to make them too often. Too much haemoglobin would use up all your iron and cause something called **ANAEMIA**.

So we know **exactly** how much you need, your body has an oxygen monitor.

Your kidneys are responsible for making sure your blood is clean and healthy. They also measure the oxygen level in it.

When the oxygen level drops, the kidneys send a messenger to the bone marrow.

That messenger is called **ERYTHROPOIETIN** (or **EPO** for short). It tells us to make instructions for more haemoglobin.

Emergency!

EPO is sometimes used by sports competitors for making extra red blood cells to help them win. It's against the rules, though, so if anyone finds out, they could be disqualified.

As soon as EPO rushes in, the builders in your bone marrow come to us in the HBB gene. They need the instructions for our boat.

But there is no room in the nucleus for a booklet or video guide.

Morning! Can we have the instructions, please?

Yes, of course. Here we are!

We can see that, thanks. But where are the instructions?

We form the instructions instead.

It's a great space-saving trick. Your Dinky Amigos are the instructions for the haemoglobin.

The secret is in our sequence – or how we line up.

This is how it works:

We all line up in a row (that's the sequence bit). The builders must then begin by separating us into groups of three.

The first group of three are the instructions for the first part of the haemoglobin.

 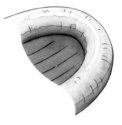

The second group of three are the instructions for the second part of the haemoglobin.

The third group of three are the instructions for the third part...

...and so on until the builders have the instructions for all all the different parts.

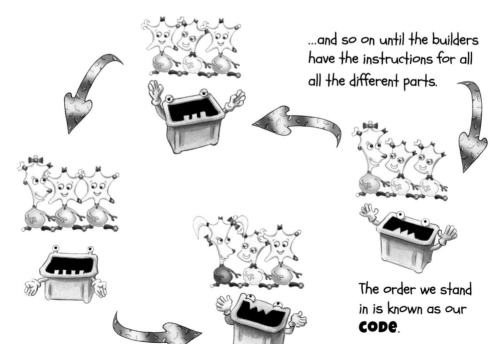

The order we stand in is known as our **CODE**.

The builders have to put all these pieces together in the right place to make the haemoglobin. Have a go at drawing it using our code from the previous page.

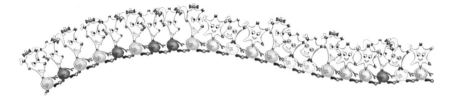

Take the first set of instructions (the three Dinky Amigos at the beginning of the sequence) and draw the picture of the matching haemoglobin piece in the box below.

Draw the second piece of the haemoglobin with the instructions coded for by the second group of three. Now draw the third piece, then the fourth and so on.

Keep copying the instructions until there are no more groups of three left. Don't forget to add the iron to your finished boat!

How did you do?

Did your haemoglobin look a bit like this one?

The builders are really good at this. They can make anything we tell them to and know exactly where each piece goes. They are a bit forgetful though.

We must give them the instructions **every time** they need to build a new haemoglobin. They can never remember themselves.

This is what we do inside your body every day, just like all our Dinky Amigos ancestors.

The Dinky Amigos' ancestors go way back

You got us from your Mum and Dad, who got theirs from their parents (your grandparents). Your grandparents got theirs from their Mums and Dads (your great grandparents). Your great grandparents were given Dinky Amigos from your great, great grandparents, who got them from your great, great, great grandparents. They were passed down to them from all of your great, great, great, great grandparents and even more greats years and years ago in your history.

(Hundreds of thousands of years. No one knows exactly as it was so far back in time.)

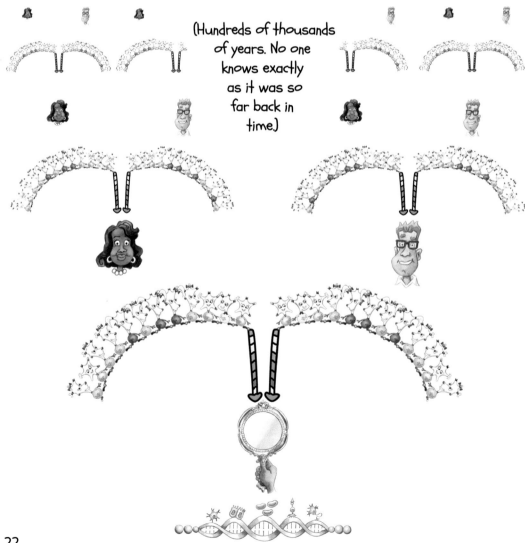

Dinky Amigos have been giving these instructions all day, every day, for each new baby that has been born since your family started hundreds of thousands of years ago.

Now that your Mum has given us to you, we start doing the same thing.

We line up in the usual way:

The builders come to us for our code, ready to make the haemoglobin.

Iron from your ferritin store is then added to make it red and give Oxygen something to do.

But there's a problem.

In order to deliver Oxygen to your body, your red blood cells must travel through some really thin tubes known as **CAPILLARIES**. They are extremely tiny, so your red blood cells need to be tiny too.

So tiny that there isn't enough room for the globin, the iron

and

us.

We have to **leave** the cell!

Once we have gone, the iron can be added to turn our boat red and make haemoglobin.

If anything goes wrong now, the builders can't come and ask us anymore. Fingers crossed everything goes to plan...

Our red blood cell sets off for the lungs without us.

But once Oxygen sees the iron,

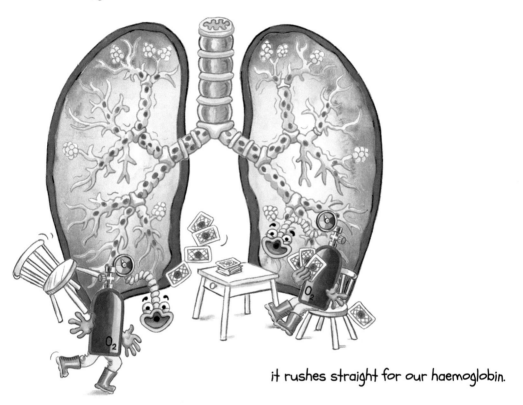

it rushes straight for our haemoglobin.

Maybe our erythrocyte doesn't need us after all.

With Oxygen in our haemoglobin, the red blood cell leaves the lungs and is carried in your blood throughout your entire body, ready to help your organs.

As it travels, Oxygen gets bored of the iron and starts looking for something else to do.

Its new favourite toy is called **CARBON**. There is lots of this in your organs. When Oxygen spots the carbon, it rushes off and leaves our haemoglobin empty.

Other Oxygens in your organs are already playing a game with the carbon.

Scientists call this game carbon dioxide.

Your organs don't like this game and send the carbon dioxide away. When Oxygen leaves, our red blood cell takes the carbon dioxide back to the lungs and swaps it for more Oxygen.

When we jumped out of the cell, we left some reminders for the builders, to help jog their memory. It allows them to keep making the haemoglobin for about 12 weeks.

Then they completely forget how to build it and we have to start from scratch in the bone marrow again. But we've got ages before that happ...

EMERGENCY!

What..?
Our red blood cell
has only been
gone 10 days!

Why would EPO be asking us to help make more so soon?

Your oxygen levels must have got too low.

Whilst you wait for more red blood cells, you will be feeling really tired.

We immediately give the builders a new set of instructions.

They finish the boat.

The iron gets added.

It picks up Oxygen from your lungs and sets off for the rest of your body.

HELP!
It's not **working.**

But before long we get another message from EPO.

It turns out that  everything was fine when Oxygen was delivered to your organs.

Then, when **Oxygen** got out,

carbon dioxide got in.

But the carbon dioxide players weren't looking where they were going and tripped over something.

Sticky stuff flew **everywhere** and **burst** our boat!

Even worse, though – the sticky haemoglobin turned your red blood cell into a funny C shape, making it look like a **SICKLE**.

Now these sickle cells don't work properly anymore.

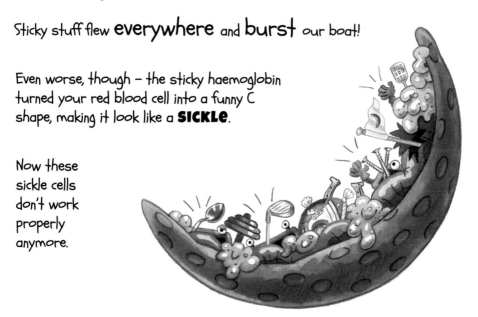

Dinky Amigos have all been doing this for ages. The builders have been doing the same thing too and they are really good at it. We didn't realise anything was wrong.

Well, nothing for it but to try again.

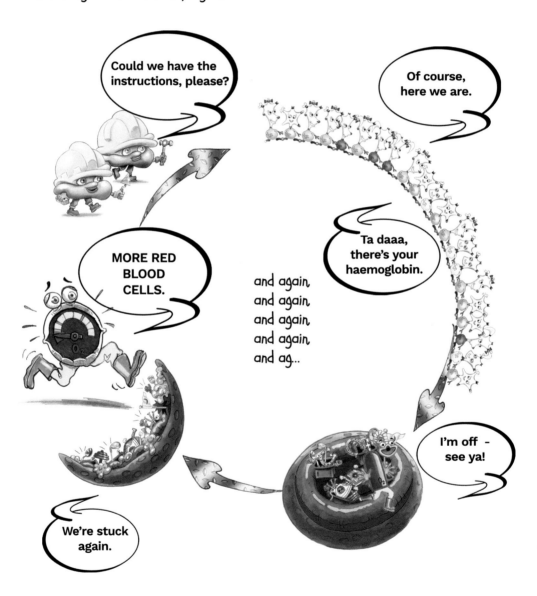

This is just crazy. Why won't it work?

None of us know what else to do. We just keep giving the builders our instructions and they keep making the haemoglobin.

Everything is fine until Oxygen leaves.

Then everything sticks together, your red blood cells sickle into a "C" shape...

...and get stuck

Your blood vessels start getting clogged with these misshapen cells.

Misshapen red blood cells in your **blood vessels** are a nightmare.

Your blood vessels are long thin tubes which help the Oxygen in your red blood cells reach every single part of your body. These tubes are thickest around really important organs like your heart and lungs. The further away from those organs they go, the thinner your blood vessels get.

Your blood flows really fast through your blood vessels. Each red blood cell can whizz round your entire body in about 60 seconds.

Sickle-shaped red blood cells can't travel fast enough to keep up and get stuck on the sides of the blood vessel.

If lots of them get stuck in the same place, they form a big clump. This causes a **CRISIS**, which is very painful. Really big clumps get in the way of Oxygen deliveries too, making you extremely tired.

If this happens you might have to take medication to break up the clump.

Misshapen red blood cells in your **spleen** could be a disaster.

Your spleen is an organ in your body. It is part of your immune system and helps your body defend itself against any bacteria or viruses that might try to make you ill.

It also removes old or damaged red blood cells. The iron is recycled and the rest of the cell (including our boat), is thrown away.

Because your red blood cells are damaged so often, your spleen is really busy removing them. It doesn't have time to properly protect you from infections.

If your spleen gets too busy, you may have to take antibiotics to help your immune system prevent any nasty diseases.

We have to check everything.

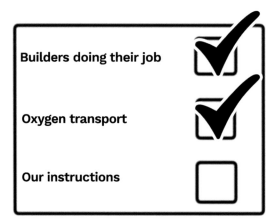

Builders doing their job	✔
Oxygen transport	✔
Our instructions	☐

Remember the blood they took from your heel when you were born? The results are back – and we're in trouble...

I say chaps – something seems to have been swapped.

It seems that Tristan is standing in the wrong place in our sequence. Our cousin Ariana should have been there instead.

No wonder everything is the wrong shape. There was a mistake in our instructions for the haemoglobin.

It turns out that Tristan got confused and ended up standing in Ariana's place in our sequence. This means that the builders read the wrong instruction.

This is what our code **should** look like in the HBB gene:

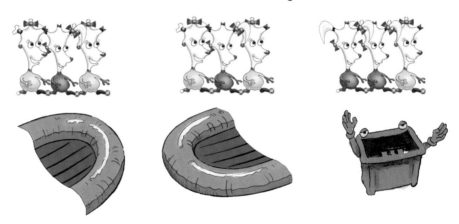

but after the mix-up, our code **now** looks like this:

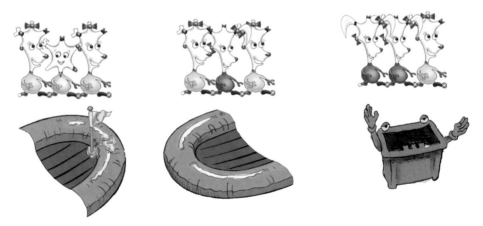

Scientists call this a **missense mutation** as the new sequence still makes an instruction that the builders can understand (just not the right one). They also give our mixed-up haemoglobin a new name: HbS.

Unfortunately, the new instruction tells the builders to change something on our boat. That must have been why the carbon dioxide players tripped over and burst it.

But, wait a minute. I've just thought of something!

Even though one haemoglobin is broken, we have a second chance to make one that doesn't get sticky and pull our red blood cell into the wrong shape.

Remember you have **two** families of Dinky Amigos living in the cell nucleus.

Both of those families have an HBB gene.

You have **one** HBB gene from your Mum and a **second** HBB gene from your Dad.

We now know there is something wrong with our HBB gene – the one you got from your Mum.

Tristan has swapped places with Ariana. This means the builders have the wrong instructions.

But your Mum didn't know anything about it.

Scientists call this a **FAULTY GENE**.

(Honestly, that is so rude. It could have been an accident.)

That makes your Mum a **CARRIER** for this faulty gene. It just means that she has an HBB gene with the wrong Dinky Amigo in it, but that probably won't make her ill.

"Carrier" is definitely not a Greek name. Someone could have made up something a bit more exciting.

I mean, your Mum carries the faulty gene in her cells, so she's a carrier.

Get it? Carries, carrier. See? No imagination!

But what about the **Dinky Amigos** you got from your **Dad?**

They also split into 23 chromosomes, with the Dinky Amigos in the HBB gene living at Number 11 too. Some of them even have the same names as us – it can get very confusing!

Their job, in the HBB gene from your Dad, is the same as ours. To help make the haemoglobin which takes oxygen from your lungs to the rest of your body.

These Dinky Amigos also line up in a sequence to give the builders their instructions.

As long as Tristan hasn't swapped places with Ariana in this gene, the builders can make a haemoglobin that doesn't get sticky and cause your red blood cells to sickle.

Then you would have two different HBB gene sequences. A faulty (or variant) gene from one parent and a gene with the correct instructions from the other. This is called **HeTeROZYGOUS**.

Just one faulty gene would make you a carrier too, with a condition known as **SICKLe CeLL TRAIT**.

Only half of your blood cells would sickle and clump together, leaving plenty of room for the healthy cells to get by and reach your organs.

So, unless you forget to drink plenty of water, or try to climb Mount Everest, you may never become ill.

You only need **one gene** that works.

If the builders can use the instructions from your Dad's HBB gene to construct a haemoglobin that doesn't get sticky, you don't need our faulty gene at all.

So we send the builders to the new HBB gene – the one from your Dad.

Excuse me, we need some instructions that work. Could we try yours, please?

Of course - here we are all lined up for you.

This is the code from the Dinky Amigos you were given by your Dad. Draw the matching parts in the correct order and remember to add iron to show the final haemoglobin.

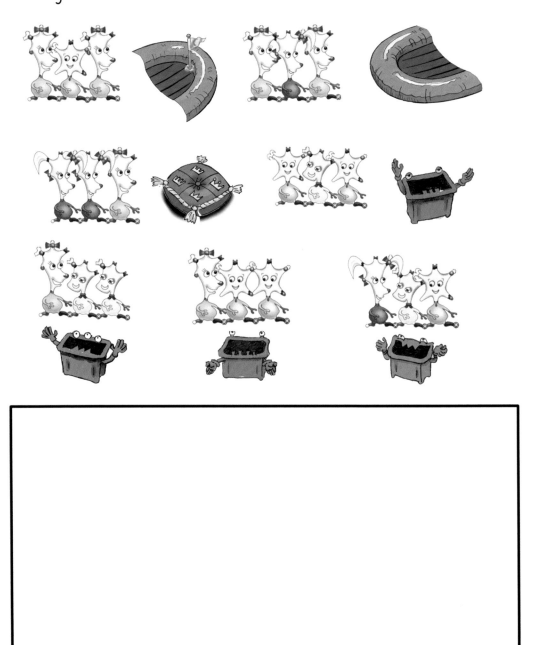

The builders have made a lovely new haemoglobin from the instructions from your Dad.

It goes off to the lungs to collect Oxygen and deliver it to the rest of your body.

But then...

Low oxygen! I repeat, low oxygen!

Oh no! The haemoglobin made with the Dinky Amigos sequence from your Dad must also be sticky.

That means your red blood cells will sickle as well, so they will still

clump together

Tristan must have swapped places with Ariana here too, leaving the builders with the wrong instruction.

That means that your **Dad** is a carrier too.

You have an HBB gene with the **same** instruction mix-up from both parents. This makes you **HOMOZYGOUS** for the faulty gene.

This is the DNA sequence from the HBB gene that your Mum gave you:

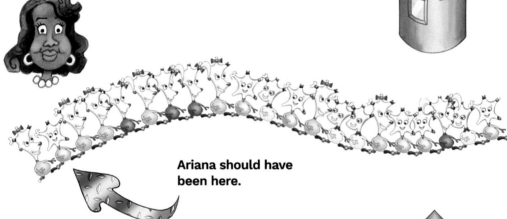

Ariana should have been here.

This is the DNA sequence from the HBB gene that your Dad gave you:

Ariana should have been here too.

Tristan has swapped places with Ariana in **both** of your HBB genes.

The one your Mum gave you and the one your Dad gave you.

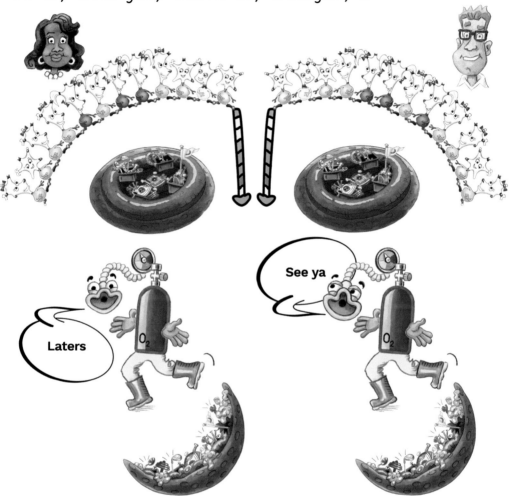

You haven't got any other HBB genes. So none of us can make a haemoglobin that doesn't get sticky.

A combination of our instruction swap and your pain and tiredness means you will be diagnosed with

Sickle Cell Anaemia.

Sickle Cell Anaemia is known as a **RECESSIVE DISEASE**. It just means that both your HBB genes need to be faulty before it will make you really ill.

The HBB gene is on Chromosome Number 11. This means that Sickle Cell Anaemia is known as an **AUTOSOMAL RECESSIVE DISEASE**.

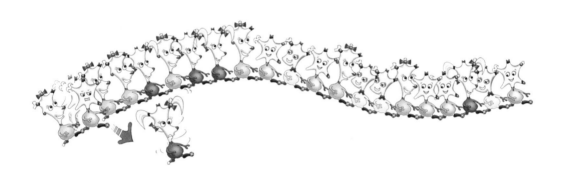

It turns out that scientists already know about Tristan's habit of barging Ariana out of the way like this. Apparently he does it quite often.

This behaviour is called a **SUBSTITUTION**.

Because only one Dinky Amigo has been swapped, scientists might also call it a **POINT MUTATION**.

Tristan sneaking into Ariana's place like that has caused a real problem – and not just in our blood cells, either.

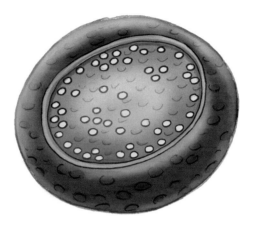

There are trillions of other cells in your body and Tristan has swapped places with Ariana in all of them.

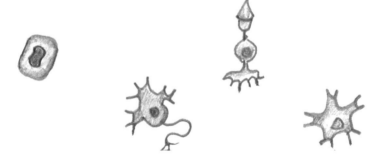

If you have children one day, Tristan's faulty instructions may be passed to them, too. There must be something somebody can do.

Scientists have worked out a way to remove the sickle cells from your blood stream and replace them with healthy ones that don't change shape. It is called a **BLOOD TRANSFUSION**.

They use blood given by generous people (known as blood donors). Tristan has **not** barged Ariana out of the way in their HBB genes and their haemoglobin doesn't get sticky.

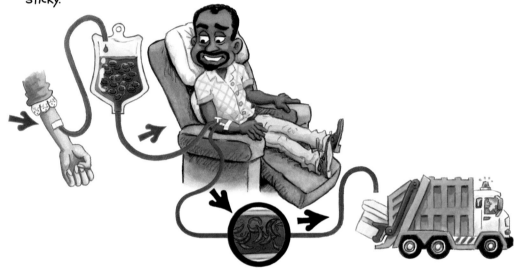

You can't just have any old blood in your transfusion, though.

Doctors have to make sure the new blood belongs to the correct **BLOOD GROUP**. Your body is very fussy and will only allow specific groups to enter. If the donated blood is not the right type, your body won't let it in.

Doctors can also replace all the blood cells in your bone marrow too.

They call this a **bone marrow transplant** (sometimes called a stem cell transplant).

All the cells in your bone marrow with the faulty Dinky Amigos instructions are replaced with new cells containing the correct instructions. Now the builders can make haemoglobin that doesn't stick

This is really good for some children and may even cure them.

Scientists are also trying other ways to cure Sickle Cell Anaemia.

They have managed to take Tristan away and put Ariana back in her original place to make a new HBB gene that isn't faulty.

They must now ask some friendly viruses – which are really small – to deliver the new gene to the cells in your bone marrow.

If this doesn't work, they have another plan. Remember the boat your Mum's blood used before you were born? That is haemoglobin too and it doesn't get sticky. Scientists are trying to encourage the Dinky Amigos to make that boat instead.

Both of these things are called **Gene THERAPY**, but it may still be a long time before they are ready for everyone to use.

But why did Tristan barge in and swap with Ariana in the first place?

He says it was to protect you from **MALARIA** – a nasty infectious disease which affects millions of people every year.

Malaria is caused by a really tiny bug called **PLASMODIUM**. These bugs hide inside insects known as mosquitoes.

Plasmodium bugs sneak into your blood when the mosquito bites you. They use your red blood cells to make lots of copies of themselves. When there are too many copies, the cells burst open and all the new bugs go in search of other red blood cells, where they can make even more copies of themselves.

So instead of helping to deliver oxygen, these bugs make you ill.
(I mean really ill. You could die.)

But if the instructions for your haemoglobin make your red blood cells sickle, the Plasmodium can't get in.

If the plasmodium can't get into the cells that sickle, it can't make copies of itself in them.

If it can't make copies of itself, it can't break open those red blood cells.

If it can't break open all your cells, it can't make you quite so ill.

Of course,
Tristan didn't
mean for you to

get **two** copies
of the sticky
haemoglobin.

Your Dinky Amigos were only trying to protect you.

You are the only person in the world for us and we hope you understand.

Glossary of Names - Part I

Anaemia
(say: AN-EEM-EE-YA)

Too little iron in your haemoglobin to entice Oxygen into the boat. Not enough Oxygen makes you really tired.

Autosomal
(say: ORTO-SO-MAL)

Any gene on the first 22 chromosomes. Both boys and girls have them.

Blood Transfusion
(say: BLUD TRANS-FYOOGE-UN)

A treatment where the faulty blood in the body is taken out and healthy blood (donated by other people) is put in. Transfusions must be done regularly.

Blood Group
(say: BLUD GROOP)

Each red blood cell carries a precise identity card, which puts it into one of four main groups: A, AB, B and O. All the red blood cells in one person carry the same identity card and belong to the same group.

Bone Marrow
(say: BOHN MA-ROW)

The location in the centre of your bones where all blood cells are made.

Capillaries
(say: CA-PILL-ARE-REEZ)

Extremely thin tubes that carry the blood to your organs. This is where Oxygen is swapped for carbon dioxide.

Carbon
(say: CAR-BUN)

Present in all cells that make up the organs of your body and one of Oxygen's favourite toys. Two Oxygens and one carbon make carbon dioxide.

Carrier
(say: CARRY-ER)

A person with a faulty gene in only one of their Dinky Amigos families. They may not know about this gene, because it might not make them ill.

Cell
(say: SELL)

The small units that your body is made of. There are over 200 different types. This is where the Dinky Amigos live.

Chromosome
(say: CROW-MO-SOW-M)

Tall houses where your Dinky Amigos live. You have 23 chromosomes from your Mum and 23 chromosomes from your Dad.

Code
(say: CODE)

The order in which each group of three Dinky Amigos must stand to give the builders correct instructions. Each group of three is called a codon.

Glossary of Names – Part II

Concave
(say: CON-CAVE)

A surface that curves inwards, giving it a bigger surface area.

Crisis
(say: CRY-SIS)

A bout of severe pain caused by too many sickled red blood cells clumping together and blocking the blood flow around your body.

DNA
(say: DEE-ENN-AY
or DEE-OXY-RYE-BOW-NEW-CLAY-ICK A-SID)

Short for (take a deep breath): Deoxyribonucleic acid. The name for all your Dinky Amigos together. (The collective noun for Dinky Amigos, if you like.)

Diploid
(say: DIP-LLOYD)

Two copies of a Dinky Amigos family in a single nucleus. One copy from your Mum and a second copy from your Dad.

Erythrocyte
(say: ERITH-RO-SITE)

The scientific name for your red blood cell after the Dinky Amigos have jumped out.

EPO
(say: EE-PEE-OH
or ERITH-RO-POY-TIN)

The messenger sent by your kidneys to tell your bone marrow to make more red blood cells. Short for erythropoietin.

Faulty Gene
(say: FOLL-TEE JEEN)

A gene with some Dinky Amigos in the wrong place (or missing altogether), so the builders don't have the correct instructions. Sometimes called a variant gene.

Ferritin
(say: FERRY-TIN)

Special cupboards in your body used to store iron.

Gene
(say: JEEN)

A single group of Dinky Amigos, living in a Chromosome house, that have all the instructions the builders need for a specific task.

Gene Therapy
(say: JEEN THERA-PEE)

A treatment that involves altering the Dinky Amigos in a faulty gene to ones which provide correct instructions.

Globin
(say: GLOW-BIN)

The name scientists invented for the boat before iron is added.

Haemoglobin
(say: HEEM-O-GLOW-BIN)

The name for the boat after it has been filled with iron. ("Haem" comes from the Greek word for blood.)

HBB
(say: AITCH BEE BEE)

The nickname for the group of Dinky Amigos that make up the gene responsible for creating the haemoglobin instructions.

Glossary of Names – Part III

Heterozygous
(say: HET-ER-OH-ZYE-GUS)

When the instructions of a gene you get from your Mum are slightly different to the instructions made by the same gene from your Dad.

Homozygous
(say: HO-MO-ZYE-GUS)

When the instructions of a gene you get from your Mum are identical to the instructions made by the same gene from your Dad.

Iron
(say: EYE-UN)

A metal found in the ground and some foods. It is essential for attracting Oxygen into the haemoglobin boat.

Malaria
(say: MAL-AIR-EE-AH)

A dangerous, infectious disease caused by a bug, which can enter your body when a mosquito bites you.

Missense mutation
(say: MISS-SENSE MEW-TAY-SHON)

A mistake in the Dinky Amigos instructions, which the builders can still read, causing problems.

Nucleus
(say: NEW-CLEE-US)

Special area inside the cell where your Dinky Amigos live.

Organ
(say: OR-GAN)

A very big collection of different cells, arranged in a specific structure, doing an important job in the body.

Oxygen
(say: OXY-JEN)

Makes up 21% of the air we breathe and essential for our body to function properly.

Plasmodium
(say: PLAZ-MO-DEE-UM)

Tiny bugs that live in the *Anopheles* mosquito and cause malaria in humans and other animals.

Point Mutation
(say: POYNT MEW-TAY-SHON)

A single Dinky Amigo swapping places in, going missing from or inserting itself into a gene sequence.

Recessive Disease
(say: REE-SESS-IVV DIZZ-EEZ)

The name for the condition you inherit when both your Mum and Dad give you a faulty gene.

Sequence
(say: SEE-KWENS)

The order your Dinky Amigos line up in. The cell builders must read this sequence in groups of three in order to understand their instructions.

Sickle
(say: SICK-ELL)

A large, curved, "C"-shaped knife used to harvest crops. This is what your broken red blood cells look like.

Sickle Cell Trait
(say: SICK-ELL SELL TRAY-T)

The condition you have when Tristan has swapped places in only one of your HBB genes.

Substitution
(say: SUB-STEE-CHEW-SHON)

The name given to the position where one Dinky Amigo has swapped places with another. This doesn't always make you ill.

Hi, I'm Lisa and I hope you enjoyed the book.

After lots of learning, I went to the University of Edinburgh (in Scotland) to study for a Ph.D. in biochemistry. Then I worked as a teacher on the Wellcome Trust Genome Campus (in Cambridge, England). I went to lots of other Universities all over the world teaching people about DNA.

The best bit was teaching biologists how to use the computer to find out all about it.

If you want to know more about the Dinky Amigos – or when the next book is ready – ask your favourite adult to sign up to the Dinky Digest at:

www.dinkyamigos.com/dinkydigest